MW01099072

Prerecorded

Poems by

Stephen Pitters

Gribble Press
Spokane, Washington
gribinc@gmail.com
hpps//:gribinc.com

Tom Gribble, Editor and Publisher
Book and Cover Layout and Design, Gribble Press
Cover Art, *Prerecorded*, by Megan Perkins
Back Cover Image, Mike DeCesare

Dedicated to the Memory of
Michaelanne Foster
May 29th 1993 - September 18th 2017

"A Magical Rainbow in the Sky
And to all she touched,
A Golden Flower!"

Guardians of Love

…Michaelanne F.

She was a sweet rose deposed,
broken from its stem,
uprooted to face a swift and bitter end.

No majestic flower
should be so undone
but she an exotic perfume was released
made to drift on the westerly air currents
to the four corners of the Earth,
to lie there in crass stillness,
devoured by time's ignoble reach.

None left behind
dare reproach the pain
that was our sorrowful gain.
In the same way is
the long acting stain,
to our hearts denied
the happiness of her
delightful smile.
Its gesture made our weighed-down life
worth the price of a gold bullion.

She marked us well with her
aesthetically creative hands
that crafted eternal beauty and hope.

Michelangelo himself
would give a complement.
Applauding her use of them
to reveal a noble bust
hidden in the ordinary clay
as is her image set in our minds
to last past this and every other day.

She isn't nor will ever be
the ghost of memories.
The reservoir of the love
for her
cures our hearts.

She is the guardian of our resolve
never to depart.

The Long March Home

The scope and fruits blossoming
within the imagination
prepares the portal
for all human activity
to find its fate

The collection, *Prerecorded*, is the result of actions and behaviors reflecting attitudes and beliefs brought forth by events during my years 35-45. This period raised the ultimate question most need to ask, "What if? and did your life ripen or rot from the time spent however long with that person you came to know?

Acknowledgements

Cover, Megan Perkins Artist—Art inspired by "The Skirmish" and "Would or Could"
www.meganperkinsart.com

Nicholas Sironka, Batik Artist, Painter, Educator:
Kenyaarts and Culture Center—
Batik Painting inspired by the poem "Together We"
FaceBook: https://www.facebook.com/batikartbysironka/about

Traci De Leon, Singer, Song Writer—Song inspired by "Guardians of Love"
"Together We" and "The Hold" https://www.facebook.com/tracideleon

Review of Stephen Pitters' *Prerecorded*

Stephen's Pitters' *Prerecorded* is a book about love and, therefore, torments—love explored, and love left unexplored, parental love, grief for a loved friend, and the simple torment and treasure that is one's own life. As always, Pitters writes with passion and a drive to explore the passions that light up his mind. "The waiting to forget/is this second beginning/with all these esteemed feelings/dancing about/like birthday gifts/waiting to be unwrapped." He strives to unwrap what lies inside his experiences, and in so doing, ensures that those experiences—good or bad—will be "Saved for all time/in the pocket of the mind."
—Jodi Hunter, Author of *Say*

Table of Contents for Prerecorded

Posing for Eternity

The feelings years removed.
Returned, no harm done.
Erica stood before me,
her alabaster beauty
akin to Stacy's
the little Rockaway Beach girl
with her golden curls
of my juvenile years.

On weekend visits to the beach,
we played fondly in the sand.
Our hands often touched,
two perfect buds sprouting.
At eleven and pure,
I adored her innocent charm.
Its goodness implored my soul.

I caught a singularly
triumphant moment in my life
each Sunday we met at the beach.

While playing in the sand,
we naively posted vows
that only eternity understood.

Erica had brought to life
the miracle I gained
twenty-seven years earlier
in those enthralling summer filled days.

Prerecorded

I regained fascinating memories
with intense clarity.
Stacy in my eyes transformed into Erica.
Her long, bright, corn color hair
swayed lazily in the mid-afternoon breeze
three thousand miles west of Queens, New York.

With young Stacy by the sea shore,
our tongues tasted the salty winds
as we frolicked for hours in the sun
that tanned her arms, legs and cheeks.

Kindred rays
highlighted hair strands
crossing over Erica's hazel eye.
The words from her pink lips
extended a friendly invitation.
The thunder of my elation again rose.
My cup filled to its brim.
I sipped.
The taste wasn't counterfeit,
but the eternal moment's unforced stay.
Our energy's synergy mushrooming
as two minds twined
and climbed a mountain of intensity.

The impact of certainty renewed.
Time and space crossed through our senses
and freed us.
Stacy and I of long ago
fed on affection without dread.

Then as now we are liberated
by unshrouded excitement
with choices made in spades.

We strolled casually to center stage.
Our fingers lightly bound.
Two decades before we hinged tender love proudly.
I was immersed by her self-made intoxication.
It distilled my heart.

Filled by the many sagging days behind me.
Wide eyed inside out
I waved the white flag
of youthful love's surrender.

I wished we were young again
with the arrival of a new day's sun
and could see past love's choice.
(Not perhaps understood, though believed in.)

After young lips dry,
age assumes its foothold
depriving one of these juicy kisses
rather than catch another soaring sun.
"Take them now
"you must if you can to heart
"Tie these titillations securely.
"Let there be no slack."
It will slow the flow
where we are to meet sympathetically
and not made to collapse prematurely.

The Move

I loved you unendingly
though it seemed
when engrossed in your presence.
We divided unceremoniously.
The loss of your intimacy
unquestionably denied the possible.

The emotional shards
afforded little self- preservation
in the meager hours left.
Closeness aborted,
fractured,
a marble slab smashed to smithereens.
Only particles resided after the impact
of the abhorrent deed
we to ourselves performed.

The guilt swallowed,
repulsed,
attempted to transform into aesthetics
the dark truth supported
as mere verbal incidental accidents.
The hearts we deformed
groveled in filth and slime
for our egregious felony.

The fatality was a powerful representation
of our outrageous vice

given by love's flight
from mercy
to extort a rushed perception.
Nothing other than our frail sandcastle
would be washed away
by complacency's wistful will.

Ruination dressed us for the exit.
The warning signs were not hidden
from our tired eyes
lowered with glances
that betrayed antagonisms.

A safer dissociation endeavored
to trump the unpleasant offerings
we wagered with brutish disinterest.

The state of affairs we initiated
stood toe to toe.
Brave warriors who slashed
their opponent selfishly
in a saucy feeding.

We were incapable of breeding
or indulging again
in what profits the heart
since it, too, was spent.
Tired to seek assistance
to repel the dragon's brimstone breath.
The floor in the home
we occupied was scorched, blackened.

Our follies could not be repaired.
The damage was costly.

We became un-heralded martyrs
who suffered inwardly from the agony
creping through us stealthily.
(The tenacious fever had absorbed its dwelling.)

The void each knew
had hoarded one's own treasure
and executed the prime directive.
"Turn the screw until it fits snugly
and chews the threads of hope."

Mongrels disposed to harm we were.
We growled.
We were the essence of a mighty hurricane
ready to assault whomever came near.
The storm between us
poured down ungraciously on our heads
each to each the enemy.
We scraped thin
the fine line of rented persistence.
Until, revelations cast forth the knowledge
that prosperous behavior
demanded courage to endure
and resolve any reign of terror
wielding its scythe.

We sat saintly on the other side of doom.
We ran to hide apart, preferably,
unenviably and suitably.

Chosen to disembark
at the appropriate depot
we each were assigned bleeding hearts
that wished to pull the nail early
from their own lengthy crucifixion.

Snow Flakes Falling

The presents wrapped artfully.
Silver bows topped them.
Surprises stowed inside
waited for the odes of the Yule Tide season
to arrive.
The one's unfastening by my imagination
contained what her bareness was about to expose.

Was I deserving
this gift freely given?
The sun-dried inlaid Polaroid memory reviewed
the facts of my extended desires.
They climbed to the heights of a three story
yellow bamboo plant.

My craving
fed on her stimulation
under the protective shadow
on the forest floor.

The result was far from offensive.
It richly defended the allegation
and compromised neatly
the pith in her needful deed.

The morning has dawned in America,
and I am now a worn tree
corroded down to its foundation.

Prerecorded

My rings are charred.
I had lain upon a crackling fire.
My energy handed over from the fading embers
stir slightly
to accost the chill.

In my Vermont, I am the tree
with my maple syrup tapped out.
Her laughter resonated serenely off
the four purple walls after the darkness left.
She was the genuine siren broker.
Her squeeze in the end
took all the juices from my silent flaccid hammer.

The New Year's Eve thereafter wasn't appeased.
At times, there just weren't enough coals
left to pulse the fire.

However, with fortune's visit,
The unnatural imitation reported for duty
and made its case stand rightfully straight
and firmly sustained the cheerful flames.

Their rampant desires now wetted.
Vocalized the 60's love, sex and rock and roll sounds.
Their band needed to continue jamming.

Deciding the Universe

Tuesday morning came,
and the dampened bed
chose not to blame the crushed silk sheets
dominated by our communal high jinx
throughout the night.
The flavor spread everywhere.
We couldn't withhold
what was instore anymore.

The blush refused to vanish
the employee
who wouldn't let go the hard work
he gave to supply her entrance.
My libidinal urges she unwittingly spurned
when fright found her coveting me
beyond her limits.
The landslide of her lascivious infatuation
cascaded opposing the prospect
of hazards, heretofore, unimagined.
Would she continue to plunge in
and accept accountability
or be the tense, skittish rabbit?

The offer we pursued
awarded us unusual perks
normally withheld from a cushy valley.
Surveying the gap,
we rushed in at a double-quick pace

over its mushy roads post haste
and emerged at a detour
to discover the relative peace
due any excursion.

Our minds previously beset with apprehension
was inscribed with confusion,
which required retooling.

Next to the country road we approached
flowed a placid stream.
We forded it over an arching bridge.
From its side rail on the water
was our reflection.
It produced a magical image of us
and reminded us of a fateful, fruitful beginning,
(Our determination installed
to keep an open door to disperse foul humors
from clogging our delicate arterials.)

Behaving madly,
we craved steak and eggs
to confirm our state of being.
Our profuse transgressions, however,
required an apology.

A deep breath could not
freshen our rubbish,
nor develop a generous collateral
to cause our estate to flourish.

To survive, we elected to return
and garnered the Kingdom of Heaven.
As persons of interest,

we blended
and bonded to the fragile claim
known as life.

To one another, we confessed,
"While in this world
do what you will
but respect me,
and I to you
will give all my love
as I do to the Good Lord above
who perpetually watches over us."

The Atonement

I sacrificed my heart to love
and to whatever feelings it once carried.
This precious gem was damaged
by its lack of use.
(Yet still expectant!)

The accidental discovery of feelings
released by a new untested opportunity
humbled the hunger of eating scraps
in back alleys and wastrel taverns.
These visitors served to satisfy
the recesses throughout my body.

"I deserve to be appreciated
and prized.
Taken at face value,
not the smudge
left on someone's back doorstep."

I tried not to forestall my worthiness
nor my self-esteem
when stretched almost to its finality.

I hung onto a primal existence.
The one certified in the contention
vested by God in all His creatures.

No illusion hunted tribute
only my love desirous of an acquaintance
on this planet with you.

You made my need
elevate the level of my stature
to equal one as elegant
and revered as you.

No queen deserves less than her king
that she may look up into his eyes
and hear her heart's saxophone play
Coltrane's "Naima's" soulful notes
that conveyed her appreciation
of impending continuity.

So here I am with my love
for your love to stay,
to which she, too, agreed
and said,
"The measure of our life onward
is forged in Tungsten steel."

The Sound of Magic

The intonations
from his gravel tuned voice
secreted unrefined passion.
They defined hard times.
His potency revealed the hidden reflections
from the passion beneath his onyx skin.
He opposed the oppressive plow.
The vexation required reversal.
It came with an unmitigated outcry
whose thunder shattered
a stain glass window
and rattled the body's noble parts
of slaves standing on the master's property.
Its turbulence capsized
and ruptured their minds' orderly progression.

Conceived as obligation,
was the soul's reprieve
from the gallows of cohabitation.

After ten years of feeling enslaved,
he sought relief from the shackles
that threw him into a maelstrom of confusion.

Laden with unjust compromises
the weight of this burden's dust
attached itself daily to his ankles, feet
and into the folds of his neck.

Prerecorded

He fought the queen of the estate unruliness
and the emotional smut she radiated.
He crunched the crud with his heels and toes
into mud on rainy summer days.
In his mind the slave owners face,
he stomped into the earth.
She didn't hear
his feet fleeing.
They splashed through the marshes
alongside backwoods roads.
The blue worn overalls torn by branches
covered his legs as he ran.
It reflected a form of living
not gone well with time
indifferent to his plight.

Each day's dread
crept through his head
and framed the right of his flight towards liberty.

The minutes of internal counseling
against acquiescence increased.
The lack of respect for her brought the roar,
and its proclamation broke open the door.
The chase to realign his stars
to fit his universe was determined.

From the long dark laces draped around his neck,
scuffed brown shoes hung.
They bumped against his chest as he ran.
The bruises barely interested him.
They were, too, important to his simple feet.
The base of those common toes
spent so much of their day

harassed by heat and clay
on stone acreages
around the big, white antebellum house.

Tender soles crunched stones
unapologetically in a mad stampede,
while crossed cords
bound the softest hide
and protected what would travel at times inside
on the cushions were these shoes'
added repose for the size twelve feet.

"These yams," he often said,
"Thumped the common ground
working and working
from sunup to sundown
steeped in poverty's yoke."

These rough feet
kept their severe stories alive
and brandished the calluses of sacrifice.
The howling was not worth debating.
They are only
irritating tales,
rumors accepted.

These old feet eluded miles of traps
and came like a caller to a Quaker's house.
A guest who dropped in
after crossing the barriers
of marsh land and stagnant water.

He had cleansed himself of her.
He wore neat brown trousers,

and an off-white shirt
carried in a blue bag.
The shined brown leather shoes
were fastened by black shoestrings
that made their way
through silver ringed holes.
These unworldly shoes would trample
any who attempted to impede their way.

Contradictory was not his reflections
of her love's ingratitude.
Though they failed to reconcile the anger
he adroitly avoided
and did not retreat
nor weep for one more day
of fighting off the vestiges
of an age-old taxation.
Love maybe blind,
but love is truly like dying
(incoherently).

Brightside

The ideal face was before me.
Her emerald green eyes
engaged mine with three meters between us
with hope of exquisite love to follow.

Her charisma nestled deeply
above her curved cheekbones.

The words she stated presented
a lifetime of fidelity to my ears.
"I am the skiff and you the river
on which I drift."

I bent my knees.
The marble floor greets them,
and I am in that moment a serf.
Later from the hunger in her heart
she again said,
"I am for you as you wish
for I must have
what your need and mine
rings in us as true."

The queen's sun long strived
to reject being eclipsed
by arrested emotions
and masked her feelings for me.
She was detained

by her remorse trespassing
and corrupting joy's reach.

A latent flower in distress
and hurt was she.
Unable to find the moist soil
in which to bloom,
the iris in its garden hates the thief
who broke the stems
that hoisted its bouquet's appeal.

A blight to the eyes of all posterity if wasted,
unappreciated, unrecorded memory
nearly swept clean
and overrun by sluttish time
seeking to hasten death.

I with love's decisive deed
retracted the execution
from the sorrow she wore
with the hope we instead may flourish
and cruelty retreat from the regal heart
for which I so deeply cared.

Come's the time that raises the mind
and the will to gain requited love
and define our oneness.

Belief made their kingdom flourish.
Its champion's
red, green and blue banner fluttered
in the wind above the castle's walls.
Nothing now withstood their arrival,
the trumpets' voices wailed congratulation.

Her darkness removed
by the sun's borne ideal
felling further doubts.
Sweet plain verses of love
she wrote to me.
Their constancy appeased
my ageless, longstanding pursuit.

"My grief," said I,
"Waited for you, for this day,
and though ages ago, I found you."
My time dwindled from the bright side
to occupy the inside
of death's door.

Serione

The seed is the truest pilgrim.
Its roots spreads outward
tasting the rich nutrients
crouching below the uncharted soil.

They make precious contributions
as did the Three Wise Men
who voyaged from far
to bring their sacred treasures
to the Holy Child.
The world's consciousness
was later filled
with spiritual form and substance.

Akin is she able with her star
instructing aided by her soul and
bona fide nature.

When her body develops,
the mind in tune
discovers the intricacies of itself
composing its own orchestrated music
in lightning flashes
that transcends into crescendos
of mystical purpose.

The richness in her energies
offsets any injunction

contrived to prevent
or intercept her natural course.

Protected with sacred gifts
the slender bud
with tender devotion radiates.

Her body and inquisitive mind
advances and expands
to share with the world's
inspirational hope.

Her contact with others
immediately betters them
with her insight.
They desire to call her friend
and to extend their hearts to mend.

Serione and I spent years of accompaniment
in glorious flight,
until her tour within the celestial gate
she had to take.
It is never too late nor too early
to achieve this fate.
(Saying goodbye, my heart
speaks of the right thing to do.)

More Than Silly Games

We were youths who sought access
then deceived its longevity.
She was earth
and I hasty rain.
I showered her domain, (uncontained).

My abrupt departure
lent uncertainty to our relationship
since I was the first to entertain leaving.
My nature minted the token spent
Sharing the liberties we used,
goodbye quelled the holler
spouting from the pit of my lungs.

The horrifying descent
splotched her black hair,
brown eyes and supple neck.
Her torment was desire deceived.

From her mouth, over and over
there was a wail
She felt the laceration of the wounded cat.
The hurt pronounced its hiss.
Seeing no alternative,
it pounced to implant its teeth
and claws into an enemy.
(I am he, who dared defile her feelings.)

"You were impossible to forget.
You made me regret
the last drop of devotion
I had to give
by skipping casually away,"
she exclaimed.

She had no means of considering
nor experiencing the pain caused.

Her thoughts and spirit tortured.
She commenced traveling
the open rugged highway
full of blatant infirmities.
These mines exploded with every memory
of him visiting her mind.

This was a drug not patented
but easily obtained.
They ferried the faltered hopes
of those dashed on the rocks
by compromised aspirations. (Duplicity).

(Tales of woe is me
and how can this be
pitched their tents
wherever she wondered.)

The smile in hello was gone.
Before there was more to adore,
we said all the good things
starting brings.
We previously shared intense quality.

Prerecorded

How stupendously we felt holding hands
with our arms wrapped about
each other enduringly.
When the morning sun rose,
we still lingered in our doze.

You were the sail
and I the wind.
How did I, in my skin,
become so dormant?
Love was faulted
and forgot how good we first were
by leaving the scar
that shouldn't have been made
at such a monstrous cost.

Fair Winds

Some sounds are more critical
than others.
A baby's first words
magnifies the role eternity has in its grasp.
The echo remains a mental trophy.
The evidential proof
says, "The heart is not static."

The ping bumps the calm.
The alarm went off
and elated madness's ricochet
in the ears open windows.
The rising decibels are a magical charm.
Faith retains access to the success.
Hope had entered their world and
imparted a dynamic ecstatic awareness.

Accidental input at times
reconfigures the outlook we have.
We are the artists enhancing
the plain, stark, white empty canvasses
with skillful use of multitude of colors.

Previously, the couple's life
had little to recommend its use.
(Nothing to assist
to define its credibility.)

Bold reds, rich golds, pastel pinks
and jaunty yellows tinctures
they used to address
the imagination's tempest.
The arrangement is suddenly
charged with excitement
and evolves into their masterpiece.
Who are these plain folks
now overflowed with profound happiness?

Apprehension will dirty your rug
once challenges win a few rounds.
Fear will not take a back seat
nor wax philosophically.
It is the boulder we push uphill
and outraces us downhill if we slip
in our imminent roles as caretakers.

At nine months
the place became a party palace.
The joint began jumping
as confidence rose
with their combined efforts
to uphold their living sensation.
They didn't reject
any ulterior motives
labeled as pretense.

The dye for them is cast,
but overtime
overran their gratifying canvasses.
The blend of colors
leaks through the wooden frame.

Their conflicts resist the control
of fierce emotional outflows
created in their minds.

The finesse they master
or yet to master
in order to progress miscarried.
The initial victorious achievement
birth accorded is sent elsewhere
like a letter posted
to find an alternate address.

The hazards of the journey
seem to manifest themselves everywhere.

Is this the fall of summer
and the winter of their vexation?

There is still a fair amount of knowledge
for them as parents to accrue and execute
to feel and not conceal with false humor.

The question at hand is
would they pursue victory or defeat?
Will this change in lifestyle
overturn and confound
their prior cultivated ease?

Better you than I
noble Gunga Din
when expected joy
turns its head the other way
for more than a day.
(Years instead they spent reloading.)

Their wants
is where the fair winds blow.
One head retains
both hands, fingers
legs, eyes and giggles all his toes.
For this view, their lives are disposed
to traverse the harsh wasteland.

Sounds Abound

I bemoan a voice stilled by the accomplice
who wouldn't invite sleep to resolve the wrath.
Quiet, alone claimed and must,
to offset the noise
of her helpless whimper.
(By itself an understated assault.)
I prayed the delectable plot would unfold:
creep nearer to confer the screech,
the great truth preached silently.

The morning chimes were muffled.
the contents of the merry tale not extolled.
My anxious thoughts of "joy" quieted considerably.

She was the vista
of an exquisite maid in composition.
(Any diamond lacked her luster.)

Her absent articulations
was the hollow voices of my grief.
I asked her, "Stay with me,"
"Stay with me."
"Be my soul protector."
"Help me to see and hear you again."
"My dearest friend,
 you are the water that quiets the fire's rage.
"Be not elusive.
"Consume my wish!"

Prerecorded

I didn't hear a rejoinder.
There was a serious ruffle.
The clamor I felt was the violation.
She didn't affect the means of approval
and held it by the craw
to snatch its privileged response.
On the contrary, she ceased to abound.

I was twirled to the ground by her silence
not again to recover my effervescent mood.

My prayer for her
was an hour's pleading unmasked
with none there to validate
the magnitude of the request.

The rumbling feeling tested the throb
that elevated my skin an inch.

I cast myself like a weight
rolled off the end of a fly fishing reel.
Before thinking,
"Do not forget to live.
"Live in this world
where reality resided
with those ruptured dreams."

My orbs refocused.
Oxygen claimed my lungs and brain.
I was able to ascertain
the old-fashioned charm of the morning glory
around me.
Their soft blue beauty made my day.

Men had a multitude of flaws
carried into marriage.
Unfortunately, they were known
before he signed the accord.
He was, therefore, left to be a saint
freed of self-reproach yet not able to repent.

The Edit

With extensive fiery strokes
their voices time after time
scorched the earth around them.

The blacken debris left behind
suppressed further advances
footsteps wish to make.

Her insistence was bold
behind her piercing stare. There was no
stop sign to ambush
the flight of his agitated passions.
They were cast into an oil pit.

Her lighted matchstick held
an unwavering ultimatum,
"Commit to serve me!"
For him to acquiesce,
he spoke mitigated syllables of defeat,
the labor in a grand retreat from self-respect.
(The tolerated curse of infamous dishonor.)

Her disturbing command
and contradictory attitude each sunrise
annulled the positive accommodation
of loving daily plots.
They each may have sewn
to induce a relevant life ahead.

Per chance,
her alteration of thoughtless demands
and a modicum of self-reflection may yet
bring to them something other
than ongoing consternation.

With stitch and yarn,
their florid ornamented blanket was woven.
Conciliatory thoughts were shared,
and the start of caring adopted.
They chose to ameliorate and to integrate
rather than the incarceration of their fate.

A fair substantive trade made gave
their mental status and bodies the unimpaired
encore they frantically assimilated
with great praise. Hallelujah! they raved.
(For them in time, the grave would add a slight waiver.)

The Second Hand Handy Man

The classic one-horse buggy
jaunted on the much-traveled,
rocky country road.

Spring had sprung.
The sounds of yellow birds chirping
entertained the air.
The two passengers were making their way
to the county fair.
The chatter between them was amicable
and pleasant, until it took a forced turn.
The horse's reins were yanked backward.
He reared up and the one-horse carriage jolted.
The halt resisted the animal's fear.
Around them—adversity rose up.

The birds heard the two people
balk at one another and flew away.
The reins left and right
were pulled by different hands
venturing to offset the buggy's swerve.
The carriage shaking refused to stay put.
The partners upheld their bickering
and attacked whatever effort
to consolidate the stability the other made.

Regarding the right course of action,
there was no cease and desist order given.

Neither let the horse's reins loose
from his or her control.

Visual glare attached
itself to the increase snarls. The
two dogs displayed for
the bone both thought was more significant
than any suitable adjustment.

Holding one's ground
was demonstrated by vulgar vocabulary
and bravado.
Compliance was not resisting
but resisting boiled over,
to defend one's individuality was pure anger.

The initiator of acts
became a one-way street.
Too often cooperation was deflected
instead of respected or accepted.

Did I require permission
to exert freedom of direction
without supervision.

"Where are you going?"
was the statement she articulated.

Was my space being compromised?
Was I losing the person I once was?
Had I arrived at the point
of having to look over my shoulder
and slink out
like Bob Ford, the coward

who betrayed Jesse James.
(Isolation and withdrawal
made better options than speech.)

The time to square my shoulders
and walk straight ahead arrived.
I was the thread stretching itself
directly through the eye of the needle.
I felt this disgust necessary to avoid
becoming wrapped up,
knotted, a ball inside
kicked around the floor.
A place
one can become too acquainted
and more unsure of their being.

(When I was young
I liked to run and run
and never stop.
Caught in the fun it gave,
and the craze girls' eyes threw at me.
Interlaced with my wilds,
what was I to do?)

(Steal and gone
before the alarm sounded is how
I solved the discrepancy.
A parted wink lent the thrill
to the stroke of completion
she or I could
with the least effort could repeat.)

Yes, fun is where you belong,
until the indoor temperature gets acutely cold.

Prerecorded

The freeze dries the skin.
Cracks on it occur
and find their ways to the heart's
pipes burst from the ice
clogging the in and out flow.

Hurry, one must save what they can
and have a second plan
to go where they truly chime
and percolate instead of remaining
projecting an advanced bleached color face
when the hearse rounds the curve
and pulls up at the front gate.
(It will have no estate
but will gladly give shelter to its freight.)

And Then Goodbye

Their hunger was left in a dinghy
to voyage wherever.
Their disagreements lacked restitution.
They received only a vanquished redress
from a closeness too deeply confined.

These two were crowded slaves
in the belly of a ship
suffering an ordeal
linked to the understated
shocking farewell;
they selected to implant dispassionately
with their fatal trips
down emotional murderer's row.

Their sickness influenced its authority
then waited for them to explode.
Nobility lost its privilege.
Desire vacated its notable capacity
to complement their infamy
and presented itself
without attributable accessory.

She does not abdicate
once the fiction is captured,
and the message extracted
with absolute assurance.
His clever mind didn't care

nor waste a fraction of tact
probing for insincerity.
(Clarity possesses the strength to
crush negativity and its intolerable strain.)

Their paladins being recalled,
have the right to apprehend,
and disperse a peaceful calm,
to reseed their soil abandoned
and left to spoil.

The Mission

I feel a song spread over and in me
comparable to a precious love retrieving
its mission worth completing.

I mean to love you
to keep you from becoming
a fragile carbon colored column of smoke
sputtering through the air
after death's mandate
disobeys life's insistence.
(Much that is still you compels
and lingers over and in me.)

I remember.
Oh! do I remember the joy
as children we had
scampering willy-nilly climbing trees
akin to squirrels in the park.
We danced, romped in unison, fluid
rivulets of a river.

Freedom flouts its own advantage.
From you, I am obliged
to find my own way,
to abandon the experience subject,
(under the circumstances)
to the impact the bullet unleashed

for me to eat,
consuming and abetting
the hasty departure
owned by my disarray.

Near Perfect

You were always morning.
Your face, a perfect,
spark borrowed from the risen sun,
which constrained cruel fate's fun.
This victory swallowed distaste,
Supplied the sweet remedy
memory uses to reminisce.

The Alignment

I felt the fertile heat.
Her coco cream body exuded
a Thanksgiving threat,
a confirmation for me.
In good mercenary conscience,
I couldn't refuse
to take advantage
and accept the challenge
of massaging her body's
intriguing message
with a decisive frontal attack.
(Aligned and perfectly entwined.)

Who Is She?

I glided, a salmon swimming in shallow waters
from what became hence nevermore.

I believed it made no difference
should her door fail to open.
What she represented was my soul:
having discovered the spite of hell,
for lack of a proper daily greeting
too often suspended
from the value love necessitated.

Had I to her become the end of a trivial pursuit?
The devil himself said,
"Is she worth burning in hell
where your remnants
are heading and will dwell?"
"The site is no chapel of divine dreams,"
Lucifer reminded me,
"Your skin will peel off in the fire
where pain resides comfortably.
"You will not be a snake shedding
its springtime mode
and elude the detriments life holds."

The torrid torture I endured
could not restructure
nor restore the love lost.
It had to be left buried outside my body

to become a needless reminder
of the superior melodies past.

I accepted ardently
the fate that came
and added insult to my heart
with a lightning bolt spike.
The massive thunderous punch split its nucleus.

"Let your steps
not leave a trace
of what you thought you found,
as a magical endorsement
for a lifetime of luxury."
"Marriage can open the earth below your feet
before you have time to flee as a fugitive
becoming a transient above
instead of a welcome guest below."

Satan not known as a friend of man
understood my difficulty.
Love was a rigor
and had a mind of its own.
It didn't evacuate smoothly from what it felt.

The mind, however, knew
certainty was not hope.
Hope was a thoughtful question
or a provocative wish
associated with a worthy cause.

Was she the drink for my plain's thirsty heart
to uncover in this life
how to exist?

My will deciphered what was true
resided in the latitude of restraint.

I expunged
her invested deceptions
and the hundred manipulative tries
melting me down into an impotent,
impoverished, vacant hollow.

(Constant truths wear the face of deceit.)

The Declaration

… Eliza Hope Bennett

She was not a wasted road traveled,
but the road
over which I squarely believed
would impart the offering
contributed as oars to my ship.
With such assistance, I may navigate the world
trekking on the waves of my soul,
discretely exploring the facts related
to bewitched debauchery.

These charitable affairs were meant
to induce peaceful gratitude
and pleasant solicitude.
They satisfied my earth days' appetite.
The fantasy for the Garden of Eden.

Written instead,
the death knell of a hellish inquisition.

The harsh synonyms and antonyms
used to fill the lines
accounted for a poor man's autobiography.

The details faltered after barking.
The words offended what defined the possible
with a grandeur that annexed satisfaction.

Prerecorded

Better had the self-same image
was able to be seen
situated in clear lenses.
Their glasses not shattered
but sealed like the bankrupt recurring feelings
inducing a pitted kinship.
One replete with careless information
frequently spewed
through discordant exclamations.

These extensions were housed
behind lackluster expectations
of falsified lyrical incantations
delivered in flat monotones.

The days of harsh battle
presented the unclear headway.
They intentionally followed
and mapped the sorrows
of misbehaving buffoons
who edited the substance
from their pulverized paradise.

(We poised ourselves for misuse
since the wise man's words went unheeded.)

(He had cautioned,
"If they can only sweep the floor
let neither enter the other's door.")

Bernadette

—The Four Tops

Bernadette my prayer is for thee,
and while alive if without you,
I'll be cleaved.
Kissed by death's degrading lips.

Bernadette, "Recall me to life!"
and let us depart from the underground.

Push adrenaline through my veins
and raise my body.
Furlough it from its grave.

Rewind the acts of old.
mold our fine souls
into inlaid gold
and fold us
with a grand climax to behold.

Your effortless ways improved life.
You safe guarded us
from the likes of a debtor's prison
where dubious women
longed to steal one's ideal dream
with honeyed assurances
designed to add dismay
and embattle the surging ordinary day.

These beasts were merely locust
searching for meat to eat.
They came.
Cast their net of untold misery.
They chose to degrade even
autumn's leafy kaleidoscope
and replaced them
with damaged artifacts
in my world if they could.
(Good fortune with poor decency
invites darkness.)

One pure as you,
I know, would refuse to implement
such loathsome conduct
by closing her door
to protect her rare virtuous richness.

My solace insured.
Evil waited
and needed to contemplate
its next debate.
Those with vacant hearts unchanged
were made to suffer.
Nothing of you to them was rendered.

They were muted
and grossly pained
before drowning in your scorn
kept them submerged.

For you and I
when all was new,
peace and time flew.

We came to be parted.
The absence mirrored death
where we joined.

Bernadette,
dying gave back what was fitting.
The stirrings time apart didn't settle.

Ticking

Part One

I need a loan
from someone who cares.
I placed a few calls.
The lines are cold.
The ringing not interrupted.
I welcome an excited voice.
One with a friendly spirit attached.
Silence was the only answer.

Where are all my friends?
Who will stand by me?

The arm of the clock ticks
as it walks quickly in a circle
but stays at no point particularly long.
My heart feels the shifting pace.
I start to lose perception.
I shuffle and lag.
I must be losing the race.
My friends are proving a distaste.

My soul scrapes along the pavement.
It becomes a course ally.

I ask street commuters,
"Can you spare a quarter or two,
to block the holes
on the bottom of these

worn-down leather shoes?"
Pedestrians see my little toe
protruding out
on the left side of the shoe.
They think but do not tarry.
There is no silver tinkling.
No clink in the iron cup
nor a swish reaching the bottom
of the black felt hat in my lap
as I sit looking up at dull hazel eyes
not caring to stare back.

Once I dug gladly
into my pockets
for the Washington induced smile
that a passing pilgrim's bill generated.

My desperation wares a tattered coat.
I am cloaked in a leisurely bareness.
I hold court seated on a grated throne.
The steam escaping from below it
both warms and insults
the skin on my bones.

Rags are my friends,
(like stealth eavesdropping)
but where are all my friends
who could deliver me
from disappointment's arrival
and the vicious laughter
of the demons parading inside me?

As I fight for hope,
will anyone sacrifice a coin or a dollar

instead of running
like a wild herd in random elegance
that chooses their own outcome to engage?

I could hardly fathom my twisted prospect.
I knew I was trapped in poverty.
The result choices
imposed by perilous living
in a defective sphere.
(This drama is a beggar's life told,
as its time scurries bye.)

Part Two

From atop a fabled sun red rock,
the mind sits bruised and beaten,
but its dedication to survive
grappled and bolstered the will
of this waning creature still.
(I am the entity dignity vacated.)

Lunging into my senses,
mind, body and spirit attacked life anew.
Attacked living
and deleted asking for any foreign assistance.

Somehow by enduring,
I held the key to the cost
and the manner, how my life should be
by exceeding the poor customs
of birth and dying,
surpassing the quality
ingrained in pursuing living life fully.
(I am who I so define.)

Fate is the trap seeking
to make perfect decisions,
such as the ones with a simple
beginning and an easy end.

(Little about life is simple.
All living things will arrive
at their contracted halt.)

(Never did I to this trial go without question.)

However, my blemishes tainted my character
and temporary lapses, made me forget
my duty to attend to the four pillars of certainty:
life,
liberty,
health
and the search for what happiness
accords:
a little less,
a little more,
a little softer,
for me to endure
and manifest
my fruitful homecoming
with death.

Goddess of Life

Regan was delivered
by the stars as a mortal blessing
to them on earth.
Her parental inhabitants quickly
claimed their inheritance,
a debt to her opulence.
Selflessness proved the vast love
they entertained in her behalf.

Regan carried the bundle of their aspirations
and firmly fashioned their globe.
Fully strapped in—contentedly so.
Her presence held them closely.
The unexpected affluence
made even the poor
equally rich in character with this tiding.

The foundations these intrinsic values bore
into their souls,
would shake them to heartfelt tears
when they observed their stars'
deliverance to earth.

Regan was a formidable power.
She was breathtaking—the properly stunning
Jewel of the Nile.

Prerecorded

She fused their destiny
till the sun decided to hide
but first it paused
for all to see her final reflection.

It was then they may ask not for pardon
when granted the shadow of their lives.
Knowing her guarantee was made in their names
and for what they were never sorry
to have lived their life, to give,
to convey her privilege.

Driftwood (Washed Up)

Part One

You are the night's brightest star,
the North Star,
the constant glimmer,
the weary traveler below seeks as counsel.
The mariner's venerable
guide to a safer port
after eluding jaw-dropping tides
climbing high
to take him down under its surf.
The boxer's violent punch
does as much to wobble his opponent's knees.

In the ensuing crash,
his face usually smashes squarely on the mat.
The blood oozes from his nose.
The black dot of his eyes
rolls backwards up inside his brow.

He lays unsure for minutes
about the lightbulbs flashing
and the sounds coming from many directions.

His mouth agape is a mass of dribble
in route to the left side of his lips.
A murky haze pinpoints his painful gaze.
His head is stuck to the canvas.
Consciousness drifts between night and glare.

He clings to this confusion,
battered and splintered,
a piece of wood in a turbulent salty sea
catering to his company.

Part Two

A man's travail is sometimes accidental.
Worldly events ripen him
That he may experience enjoyment
before eight-bells toll.

Prosperity spent
abbreviates his pot of gold.
The female's animal overflows
clutches him with her magnetism,
And she thwarts any sense of reason
he professes to possess.

His summer's ecstasy deceives
the colors of his fall,
burning hotter,
keeping him enthralled longer.

When his leaves weaken and break off,
they spiral swiftly to the ground.
They prostrated themselves
for heavy shoes to bruise.
His eyes staring aloft see only empty limbs
to salute.

His winter hurries
to negate his usual spring exuberant spree
with his cavalcade of briar roses

that imports to him their warm offerings
to test his bee-like sting,
he often used to amuse them.

However, in this go round,
his swanlike performance
gives them a hint
of what his crusty gray hairs ushers in.
The insufficient energy he has
to lengthen their ramble.

He tries chartering fuel
to extend and erect his stay.
None comes early enough
to maintain the force of his shape knife,
dulled by convincing age.
Exposed, he lays resting.
His twilight is eclipsed.

The mockingbird emerges
and offers him its dirge
celebrating his body's conversion
from the light of day to the darkness of night.

His spirit ascends (thereafter),
and he sees a friend.
It is the glittering points of the North Star
extending him the buss of its welcome.

Life's Persistence

A certain kind of love always seeks us,
even though, we have expired.
The iron will of another,
still young in years
refuses the cessation of what the drip
of the hour glass's sand rushed through.

"You left from before me,
though never from within me,"
her words declared,
"No matter the unfilled day
or days that comes calling.
"My strength's coping will defy
the night's closing in,
and uphold what there is to remember
of our past occurrences wherein we synced."
(In these thoughts, she was defiant, tumultuous.)

The lofty feats of love, we mastered,
bolstered the parameters of our life
and allowed us to rule instantly
trivial disturbances able to, heretofore,
dislodge the calmness
residing in competent hearts.

Their strong steady minds also reviewed
many inward and outward assaults
linked to hunger's nocturnal revelry.

Prerecorded

We loomed beyond the mundane
pushing to the margins
what love seized
and filled with much ardor.

How delectably persistent are those dreams.
Their steam even now allows you
to subdue me earnestly,
she confessed, from the enclave of your grave!

Roots

Nadine and I stumbled hopelessly.
The relationship got colder
than a winter's late frost.
Her imperial bearing
in our tender years together overcame anyone
when she entered a room.
The gloominess there ceased immediately,
and the song "Summertime"
when the living was easy came on.
She was outright sizzling,
refreshing. There was nowhere else to go.
We gravitated to each other.
We had to close the doors for protection.

A full blown public health hazard
with a mission materialized.
Life as we had known it fell under the patronage
of the Four Horsemen of the Apocalypse.
From each, we withdrew for life's sake
to compose the lyrics of separation.
We were one a time ago
but emptied our inner wealth
resembling a shelf rifled in a packet store.
Our supply of resources cancelled.

The small cloistered affections
convened in fairer weather with adoring touches
of flattery lost their importance

and decisively withdrew payment on the rent.
Proverbial tirades emanated
from dawn to dusk.
Bygone cheers found us here
at these straits
savoring only contempt.

Rejection was the cost
attributed to these two confused lives.

The calendar's jagged edge
not contesting their cruel fate
turned over into a following new year.

More days for deceptions discovered
for them to unleash profound malice
were esteem once dreamed.

We barked distasteful ridicules face to back.
Twisted the unjustified work of our hearts.
Love sank to Laurentian depths.
(Dislike was appeased nevertheless.)

We could have appealed
all our sins be granted peace.
Since the mind can find its own place
and was able to make a heaven of purgatory
in the vein of the capacity to rebound.
Tears caught descending,
mixed with rose petals,
fermented a congenial fragrance,
revived the fallacious dream believed.
(Fear will gain when a lie profits
as did their early spring.)
Gentleness withstanding inadequacy

toppled the indentured harm full blown
and forgave the bruising words their lips
upon each had carried out.

Scarcely was there
a smile till then
applied to these faces meandering
along such an erring path
harassing each with loathsome speech
to the brink of dust for them to reach.

Defeat waited,
bellowed an evil laugh
ready to extract the price
bowing heads made
on a thick course rope
pinching shut the eyes narrow slits.
Watery grief left to run down the face
after the sudden jolt snapped the neck.

Their fragile sympathies
beyond a doubt were impeached.
But a defiant resilience
undid mortal's flaws
to transform their wayward wickedness.
Inspired cruelty crumbled.

Positive thoughts restrained them
from procuring a total breach
whose reach were fingers groping
at the neck to provide eternal sleep
rather than an enlightened bridge
that spans the bay
to keep their crossing in play.

Prerecorded

The irresistible offer
seized their minds
through its revelation
of how amazing they had been
when their life sang before it hit
the feel of a horrendous traffic jam.

Pleased, they consumed the direction.
Cleansed were the breaths of each
with pleasant speaking.
The nurturing returned growth
to dictate its mission above ground.
Their roots for posterity appeared sound
to assist their life with its undertaking.
(Understanding is the perplexing,
emotional occurrences unwilling to contradict
any private intellectual opinion.)

No Day but Today

—Idina Menzel

She was everything necessary
to define a perfect vessel,
who is open and full of love
with the capacity of giving as does
the Lord above to His earthly creatures,
hence, they knew
and saw the road leading
to what sacrifice appoints.

Forced restrictions
akin to prohibitions tasked her mind.
Regret filled her coffers.
Much of herself, she served-up.
Reminiscent of hot food from a grill
on a paper plate
to those whose demands appeared unceasing.

The sky fell, and released
her unpleasant bitterness.
It oppressed and taxed
her unnatural sensitivities,
squashed her devotion,
renounced its high regard
and with a sword spilled the blood
of untamed barbarians.

She enacted her abdication
to improve her advantage
when tolerance in her view
only furthered relational annoyance.

The inmost scars she covered
to bridle her negligence.
She originated supposed elegance
for the life de novo.
Posing,
in the same way as, autumn days that trolled by
took their turns to convey
freshly minted sunsets unsoiled.

She was substantially destitute internally.
There was no place she could truly escape to,
from her own dreadful deception.

The Good Earth

I want to believe in life's closing indulgence
before death places
its cold hand upon my throat
and stalls the beat of blood
through my heart.

The battle to live
brings me the imperative of forgoing
the dawn of another second's greeting.

I lay rigid,
desiccated bordering on rejected meat
on an iron six-foot slab.
I was resolved in my destiny's hold.

Welcome Back

Their strained amused look
was the alarm
of their troubled hearts.

Boredom newly inaugurated
converted the promises
wrapped by their golden rings
into scrap metal.
A disgraceful affront to their splendid first dance
at the wedding reception
where the band played on into the night.

Their tired red eyes flashed laborious blinks
to each other under the black night sky
as the stars stared down from above
the giant oak tree
on the lush green lawn.

They were composed into oneness
and kissed sweetly
being in years twenty and four.
They fantasized of nothing more
except to underscore the evening
by self-perpetuating after the celebration
to increase their own musical chords.
(The patience of the young
thought all things will endure.)

Their thoughts saw clearer now
how a great many years ago
their world began to spin.
Their travesties hid their inattentiveness.
Their faults obscured all
but the half inch irrational spikes
used to draw the drops of plasma.

Their absence of control truncated
their deification when they tried
to please themselves every day
in any way possible.

Their fraud demands
their exploits endure unfailingly.
It was the clever merchant
who offered her his constancy forever
with one finger crossed over the other
behind his back.

Without her knowing,
the key in the lock pried the door open.
His frenzied dash to the 2018 year
Mazda car was successful.
His right foot covered the accelerator,
and the metallic-silver sport car's engine purring
was the last thing she heard and saw
from the slightly ajar bedroom window.

The trail of its grey smoke detailed the roadway
from a distance.
The rush it created ripped apart
the inside of her head
as she lay crying on the bed.

Composing herself she thought,
"There but for God's mercy go I.
I dare not wonder why,
except for pity sake."

"My strength of character
will accept this break up.
All that is good
will always come again,
and I will be here
stronger,
to call it friend."

(She burrowed her head into the pillow
and started the sleep that refreshes.)

Floating in the River

The piercing mixture of her blue green eyes
stabbed left and right
combed the ionosphere for me.

(They dismissed all others
previous extended stay.)

The white foam dripping from her lips
resembled a string of silver pearl beads.
They disgraced her impassive stride
parting her mind from its reality.

Unbalanced and wavering
she became detached.
The same as a life boat unstrung
from its mooring.
With the chain unfastened,
the hull ran aground on the rocks.
The cargo spilled out making its way
like blood from a sliced body.
Seeing her wrecked in selfsame shape,
it drew forth my sorrow and disbelief.
I scrutinized my own mind
to discern the certainty of her calamity.
I needed to mend the gore
and strained as I swam to reach
the other bank of river.
She appeared an illusory form
standing on the distant shore.

Hope was faith.
It had the means of acquiring again
the wayward skylark's
imprisoned depths.
Compassion racing touch in time,
took hold and released joyful news instead.

Her loving ways returned,
outdid her accidental mania.
Assuaged,
she was a tasteful beauty again
and valued for her intensity of flavor
identical to the taste of a Robert Mondavi Reserve:
$150 dollar bottle of Cabernet Sauvignon wine.

Feeling's Magic

A good day is one without fear.
Put it on like a cloak and I can explore—
give cheer to my elementary feelings.
Assured the miracle's existence is real,
more than a onetime condition
for all who wish to affirm firmly
the courage it deposits to our lives
leading us to become aware
of how we participate in God's good graces.

Answering

Part One

I am the stranger, the revealer,
whose excavation exposed your gold
not unlike a vane so long obscured
by someone in poverty,
in need,
looking to succeed,
eliminated the metaphor with a smile.

Part Two

I freed my obstructed anger
with the fervent respect
that routed fear
and halted idle aimless adventuring.

It gave me a glimpse at eternal peace,
the positive vibes hope adores
and death ignores.

Part Three

Fortunate rather than wise are you
if meeting joy
steals your every breath
and wields you like an evergreen tree
hewn from the earth's grip
by a staunch wind
and completely takes
the blessed you give asylum.

I can only ask the tremor
and aftershock not die therein.

Part Four

I never knew my heart before I met you
or realized everything
centers one's existence,
one's universe,
is the wound in love's heartbeat
driving me never to retreat
from what you do for me.
What you do to me.
What you are to me.

Part Five

What is, is
and you are everything
That never is…
That never,
never gives.
You are always,
always for me,
always with me,
always forever in the very most of me!

Without an inkling of doubt,
I know.
Know this proof is you!
You are my life.
The occasion I rise to meet
and subsequently,
kneel at your feet to greet.

Prerecorded

Put me on.
I am your coat,
a cloak
that keeps you safe and warm.
Pull the alarm if need be.
Swiftly I will return
and spur your dream.
Focus its image
into a radiant portrait.
Hung for our hearts
to make daily conversation with,
rather than shunning the approbation
akin to Dorian Gray's
death filled eyes
at whom we dare not stare.

Despite insecurities
lurking in smoky times
when lights dim
and extinguishes our profile
given to an obtuse pretext.
Pain has its purpose to rue
and in a flash,
it makes good in us disappear.

I nevertheless with hopeful exigency
as love does through the mire.
Discover skillful means to overcome anxieties

instead of moaning
the same as a child.
The level of my casualty is my decision
to pretend another such as you exist.

I detect this hapless sickness
as the greatest lie ever instituted.
There is no other in the world for me
and no other such as thee.

The flashbacks only multiplied my agony
and puts lame characters in rewind
adding pounding musical sounds
to the score that shatters equilibrium.
It scandalizes the recollection of she
who so thoroughly furnished me
with inherent stillness.

Our hearts on this earth
meticulously intertwined
could not be disjoined.
We would duel across the universe
for the sake of the other.

Is she now really gone?
Was here before?
How much can someone feel
before turning cold as steel?
(Memory if stilled
is interrupted belief.)

(Am I insane?
Did my brain hear you call my name?
What reality do I seek to entertain?)

Confusion reigns over me.
Time needs to be remanded
to renounce the devil
who declared war
and mangled our lives
denying us
any semblance of tranquility.

We have been hurled like a meteor
its tail aflame
through the black speckled galaxy's
inept to plot a course to pilot.

(Certitude also dances with vagueness
and jeopardizes dreams.
Steals them with deception
designed to impede what only time
could make succeed.)

History in dire straits required a rewrite
an alternate ending to record,
love could and did triumph
by deposing each
and every repulsive deed,
which broke where beauty rested.
Ejecting us to drift unattended.

We sometimes envied people
for what we think they have.
The curious thing is
they may not have had
anything of real value.

Save the quest to be prerecorded.
Saved for all time,
in the pocket of the mind.

Prerecorded

I saw you once;
you found me twice.
Perhaps you will remain
behind my eyes this time
where the plastic celluloid negatives
refused to fade.

Relativity

I cannot turn you off.
Your hot metaphors overwhelm me.
They burn the corridors of my mind
and peal the skin from my tongue and lips.
The constant torrents of mentally
disputing conversations
is a faucet gushing out
a perpetual surge of water
filling a hundred barrels per minute
with overwhelming pressure.
The last lazy drop—
the terminal tap will cause the barrel to implode
in much the same way you take hold of me
with the rushing thoughts you incite
a rampaging wild fire
charring the very fabric of my consciousness.

The devil collects his place in me
though we may not agree.
He aids my head to rotate 360 degrees.
I have no exorcist to command his attention
or make him desist.
I am dazed caught in a fright.
I raise my fingers.
They pull and thug at my hair.
The follicles scream being plucked.

I cannot recede
while these warring sentiments yell.

Prerecorded

I confirm favorably their plight
tied to their desiring request
for love's fulfillment and affectations.

The exuberant energy consumed
is relative to the excellence
attributed to their objective.

Should that fail,
and we not weave into oneness,
I will dissipate and be irrelevant
to the heart's cardinal demands,
to invest, invest in faith.

Childhood passes in fractions of minutes
and readily defers to its moments
of illusive contributions.
What's left to recall is a blur,
a chuckle.
The difference made is illegitimate.

The excited emotions
beat randomly through my heart
leave me to guess
whether or not
they are of crucial importance to you.

Without ceremonial certainty,
I, therefore, must refrain
from the undertaking
of living or dying justly.

Would or Could

On the walkway
between land and water
where people stray,
we met on a bright spring day,
and a thousand affable words
bid us stay.
Stay and watch if innocent feelings roam.

Her aura confessed as much.
Her intimation likewise said she was unaware
of the sweetness—
her intonations ceded.

She confided in me with a mellow ease,
innate conventions,
explicating, love given,
love expelled,
tossed to the winds over time
for unfathomable crimes and misdemeanors.
The self-recovered in the fray
of anticipated adventures.

I was led by inquisitiveness
and the look of her arch-shaped mouth
and pearly white teeth
releasing amusing words.
They deluded yet complimented
her slow bodily turns

whose selective gestures
induced the type of happy laughter
enjoyed coyly
at New Year's Eve gatherings.

Frenetic enthusiasm
pounded the pulse of my imagination.
One's thoughts were less than reserve.
Though I invested
joules of energy to remain so.
The minutes in discourse had sped pass.
Gentlemanly form required
the proper rationale to recuse oneself.
(In her paradise,
would I be crowned?)

The bay miles and miles away
had called her. Work is the perpetrator
of many sad goodbyes.
We would resume our minutes
Whenever a chance encounter
allowed it to happen.
We saluted.

I will with my ordinary eyes
look upwardly, hopefully,
and not cast aside
another single day
where you again may saunter by
and shed your winsome smile.

I was the first to walk away before
without thought; not knowing
this day would shine on us,

and the loneliness of separate paths forge
to fill us temporarily like the center
of a fluffy chocolate—
Parisian cream pastry.

A few trials deep inside,
we both had.
The heavenly parts of you
here stole bits of me,
especially your carefree heart's smiling face.
Would our fingers again wave goodbye?
Have the best parts of us,
our hearts, fleeced of more words
be apt to assist crossing a new divide?

The light of day brought a message,
"Sometime again
we would rejoice."
The wait to forget
was this second beginning
with all these esteemed feelings
dancing about like birthday gifts
waiting to be unwrapped.
Waiting to be set free.
Unlike before,
when we casually closed the hour
absent of fanfare after we met.

Today is on this teal covered bridge
for us to share
and declare to the future
what we must adhere to.
Take the present
as our stake on earth.

You found me again.
Now bind me
as a close and trusted friend.
Stronger than the wind
that hurries by.
We were meant to strive
and not tarry again
from destiny soon to mark our end.

Your florescence was a meteor.
The red-hot star raced
to announce,
"Will you stay with me,
here and now
or somewhere else along the torrid way?"

Say, "Yes."
Say, "Yes."
and contest with a keen flurry
the rest life may offer.
Consume this prospect
deriving our best
that we have peace
in our rest.

(Requiescant in pace)

Into the Ocean

In your sight,
I am just a shadow
who walks the streets
in search of pleasant company.

Take me into your view,
not your rear view.
Make what is my reverie.
(For me, absolutely crystal.)
Your sparkle dazzles my brain
diverting it from darkness.
Any such attempts to impede
the niceties by inches or seeks to unseal
the mind from the heart—
the soul from its duty
to continue inspiring cognitive reality.
I'll mash ruthlessly that empty, lonely feeling
and howl confessing to the brutal
throbbing of obscurity.

Where is my company?
Are you here to disarm the scowl?
I have been plagued with
and later bludgeoned by me.

My laughter is a recoil
comparable to a drunken sailor
adrift on land he has no need of.

Where is she?
Is she the substance
I might come to believe
assembles the earth's progression
towards a nirvana?
My footing knows only the moving sea,

"Steady as she goes
calls him to the bridge of the boat."
He sees one thing.
The entire pristine starry sky,
asking him to proceed,
unblocked by steel buildings
peering over concrete
under noisy covered asphalt streets.
There he bid himself not go.
His face and wind-swept hair
is splashed by the salty foam
waves attacking the sides of his boat.
Standing tall, the sailor's guiding words,
He hears, "Oh captain, my captain
our fearful ship is strong,
and will take us from sea to shining sea."

A Portrait's Message

Her shimmering chestnut colored hair
was far-reaching.
It stretched well below
the curvature of her spine.
The soft mane rested like a shawl
and covered her shoulders
against the brisk breeze
wanting to camp on her back.
Its swaying motion
made an S-shaped swarm.
To the passing pedestrian,
it was an immediate attraction
waiting only for her to stop
and shake her hips and do the Twist
the way Chubby Checker taught us.

She did stop; her jade eyes
looked back into mine
and sent forth un-encrypted paragraphs
of coercing sympathies.

Her baritone voice invoked a welcome
reminiscent of a childhood
friend rediscovered,
who quickly shared
guiltless behaviors.
The conversation proceeded
at an attractive pace.

My attention to her overall substance
alarmed me introspectively.

What was, wasn't
and what is, is at fault if continued.
But why?
My agenda had no preplanned directive.
Being with her,
the flow in chatter,
traveled in the style
of the Clark Fork river southerly migration.
We looped in and out of information.
(Apparently unguarded.)
Her sleek golden calf
and well exercised sculpted thighs
sat poised as though modeling
for the eye of Vogue magazine.
They were not easily dismissed,
nor were those ten-fingers
with nails impeccably manicured.
A reach to touch or hand holding suggested
a hand in hand familiarity.

Accruing this level of knowledge
had no precedence.
Her ivory teeth, ruby lips and silky tongue
safeguarded any allusion
to administer such a dispatch
or explicit goal.

My retrospection
entered a state of self- indulgence
that led to insipid gallantry
due to the flavorful

increasing slow developing vibration
her gate restricted.

My stomach's churning
sent an alarm to my burning loins
that had no decision was to be made.

My tepid, wary feelings
or her appropriate neutrality
constructed a wall
we couldn't and didn't scale.

Something, whatever it was?
Was nothing more than
sitting together under the sun
in amicable discourse.

Some days are just days
that ended similar
to their beginnings
free of drama—unspent.

The Skirmish

Her warm tender facial expression
recognized the strength of her charm.
She seldom wasted it to capture a man.

She saw me sitting
and knew we could ignite.

Approaching closer, she conveyed a
swell of attractive vitality
masked in soundless reverberations.
They began speaking to me.
I didn't skirmish with their intensions. I allowed
her sculpted curved alabaster mouth
continue with its offer.

She kept the truth hidden
with its inevitable constructed barrier
men and women have between them,
after all, the make-believe was over.

Her teaching skills
laid bare the things
a mother didn't want a son to know
early in his days or nights frolicking.

I was inclined, nevertheless, to inquire,
climb the ladder to knowledge
and examine her tenets.
She was responsive and happy to be so.

I left my heart beating
outside her door.
My mind on fire
as I stepped across its threshold.

She was the experience
of a desperately dangerous,
salacious feast,
Rather than Prince Charming
cavorting with a dreamy Sleeping Beauty.

Everything I previously heard
or read about women's altruism
was a whopping lie,
because I didn't care
when I was with her
stealing, dealing and dreaming.
Praying for more chances
to restore my first encounter
in the lair with an enchantress zest.

The devil was real.
I unquestioning
made my deal
to extend my need for her.

I sniffed her ebony hair
through my nose
and tasted its extract
at the base of my throat.
I was the bait,
hooked and eaten by the tuna.
Swallowed whole
was every inch, of me,
down to my curliest.

Prerecorded

"I loved you more than I need to live,"
I heard her say before she left.

I couldn't ask for better words
inscribe on my tombstone.

I had from her learned to be a man.
No mere girl could later survive
or dare to undertake my understanding.

Hope was the one in a million
cost she inflicted.
Now it persecuted me.

Second place, with great effort
by the merest chance
can ultimately win the race
should my prime undergo
a modicum of its prior fire
and have me yet be the
that contender—
more to her
than just a casual friend
holding to a bit
of social swagger.

Circling the River

I tried thoughtfully to know
what could possibly
serve to define you.

The mystery was revealed
by the ten-year old
young knight at her side
who showed me the key
that was your felicity.
In-sync the flashes emanating
from your blue green eyes
illuminated through and through.

We met again.
Accident being our friend
on Kardong's named bridge.
The moment gave us another excuse
to extend our beginning.
Yesterday repeated itself
as did the Groundhog Day movie theme.

This rendition was a friendlier version.
The beautiful woman was open.
She radiated beams of energy and affability.
She made you want
to offer her, yourself
or ask her for something more
than a fleeting pleasurable smile
that breached your temporary gap.

I was not without
a sense of preference,
though a tinge of excitement
condoned a wish
coarsely misconstrued.

Round the river
day after day
the pink roses
on their thorny skinny limbs
staged a bright parade
with their undaunting redolence
giving pause to the many they attract.
The invitation served the quick
early morning fliers.

The post noon
walker-talker were we,
who appeared,
preferring to saunter.
The slower, closer-look option
had beauty to divert and gratify.

(The closer they became
the more they invested
in liberating happiness
through the channel
of due diligence.)

The roses by themselves
couldn't outwit
their converged opportunity.
On the wooden bench,
superior to the river,

our steps had slowed.
Two countenances fevered
made caution insist to desist
and communed not unlike the rapid
watery dance below the iron trestle
with their ever-growing friendly eyes.
The audible liquid force chortled its lines.
We disturbed provocative nuisances.
The agreements aimed
at maintaining the happenstance
while watching the river snaking movement
advised the shore
of its nips near to any bare toes.

I was not the only one
going in a circular simile,
stepping, hoping today
had the answer to fading dreams.

Who caught whom on the wooden bridge
attached over the city's named great falls
losing their wherewithal,
many it can be assumed,
(For they too)
Their cause met
and stirred a whirlpool of hope
instead of the lamentations
of bitter regrets.

Timeless faith peered
and said, "I was at a loss."
My searing, however, brought me
here to you.
I was quieted and purified

instead of hiding—
going around and down
to the river's rocky seat
that gladly took me
if such an act I constructed
was the measure of my self-imposed retreat.

One small shade of doubt
fate chagrinned,
and the obituary wins.

The strings binding
love to mind
didn't unwind
but hoisted the dying to life.
Their bond made
with her avowal to him
on the platform
of a teal painted bridge.

Should We Not Understand

She almost brushed me
passing through the glass doors
I held open for her,
a matador pivoting
with his arms fully extended
away from his sides,
palms up as the bull rushes by.

She didn't touch me.
I wished she had.
Her emerald eyes visited mine closely.
I saw the cushiony creases on her lips.
I counted them left to right.

Our momentary closeness
was infused by her active energy
trying to reach the cement sidewalk outside
where the sun shone,
on the sum of cars
diagonally parked,
except her white Lexus
nestled parallel next to the building.

Her greenish glad cap
formed a cup on her head.
Its bill hid most of her hair.
Edges of a few rust colored strands,
however, protruded from the right side.

Prerecorded

Dropping my hands,
I could have corralled her in my arms
just then without the least resistance.
Her fetching expressions said as much.
They intreated.

Her comely features
immediately grabbed my feelings
and frisked memories
of times passed.
She imparted the seeds
that defeated my heart.

Clearing the doorway, she paused.
In the twinkling of her eyes,
I had little recourse to apply
any strategic evacuation.
I was plainly upended.

Sanctuary bade me seek God's ruling
for what this game's outcome indicated.
Odious malady recounted the deception
of a Judas Kiss in her previous life.
She was healing from those trials
and doing just fine.
(Strange the quantity
and quality of private information
one imparts to another, stranger.)
Knowing how much she shared
caught her by surprise; she apologized.
I smiled. All was good and a friendship began.

(Someone of her fine character was due
the wealth stored in her compassion

instead of the torture
of forlorn bitterness
clamoring for reprieve.)

We stood there in the light of day
backs to the edifice
with lips and nose an inch apart.
The frontage petitioned us
with accelerated disregard for oversight
and mindfulness of her quaint
though rock solid Golden Rule.
"Only fools rush in
where angels fear to tread."

I was stupefied
given such courtesy,
in which to lavish
my curiosity.

She once gave
of herself to someone
and was banished to hurt's locker.
He crushed her saintliness.
She mourned
and couldn't emotionally germinate
for the many moons needed
to reacquaint herself
with the social fabric life presents.
The self-determination of a woman
let her prosper and again ripen
for another night's feasting.

I saw myself as the farmer
ready to till her field

with the hands of arduous work
if she appointed me.

(Her worth lacked narcissism
or the trail of vanity.)

An improved set of survival skills
balanced her participation
on any second attempted merry-go-round.

Her will was hers to censure
and declare the who, what, when,
how and where to journey
and construct the domain
for her affairs of state and heart
and not abdicate
to gather another's manly cheers.

I was the ferry in transit
she momentarily received to
hoist her gold green flag.
I sounded my horn
and let my dark smoke announce
I would draw near to her shore.

Her ice age was vastly reconfigured;
the land renewed from old growth
made it look hardly scraped or misused.
She was polished and shined;
A shoe repaired
with its heels in place
and buckles embossed
added elevation to her grace.

Prerecorded

In a serene, blue cotton flower dress,
she allowed my nearness to represent itself
without a tincture of speculation.

The ticks of the watch
began to run in reverse
slowing the course of our day
giving us more time to prance
when we felt the immodest stir
of emotion's flair.

Deference called
as I peered at the silver radiance
below her brow.
The thumping pulsation
beneath her skin showed
the twitch in her neck
that announced the proximity
we both advocated
as the ode to this country girl's
glimmering substance.

I would have stepped aside congenially
and handed her the path
but not my chance
to reprise feelings once allowed
like Jack Benny
who clung to his thirty-nine years
over and over
and never lost to age
predicated on unkind wrinkles.
(Make-up never disturbs one's sleep
but enhances the challenges it inspires.)

Majestic monuments
with their boldness
are reminders,
testaments of a noble effort.

From her to me,
we built a span, a bridge
comparable to the Brooklyn Bridge
that signified what the foregone lovers
could have accomplished.
As a result, their child
took her place in their lives.
She balanced everything going wrong
on either shore.
She and I,
to be more than strangers,
explored truths
not to forsake,
how to understand.

The March

I awaited the holiness
of your gentleness.
On entrance, it tenderized
and shaded me from desolation.

The personality of your complaints
were the published mass of insecurities
you were at a loss to enforce.
These disquietudes disclosed
your march to attain safety, joy
or perchance the act
sexual investigation
stole at its height.

The redress to off-set
those rough riders halting their charge
demanded a swarm of arrows to penetrate
the evil done
as a reckoning
to shield her holy feelings sent reeling
through a morass of hallucinations
to the far edge of the universe.
She needed now to reassemble,
modernize and discern
how to transform her senses
from the darkness of oblivion
to one of constructive solution.

How does one restart
without questioning the veracity
of what she saw, heard
or accepted as true
and had come to fear?
What were those issues?
Love hurts!

Love can plant a dreadful injection
into the heart and soul.
Love will break your trust
and leave you in unconscionable disgust.
It can be a monster on the prowl.
To trust it is to be whipped like a slave
taken and stripped of reverence.

What she had to offer
did not bite or sting,
rather let it ring loudly,
a eulogy for her heart
that it may go round and round
on the merry-go-round
avoiding throes before it stopped.

On the ride, I preferred
to snatch the gold ring,
place it on her left ring finger.
Have it make us one.
Thereupon, we may sing
truthfully to the soul
and experience the world superbly
in all spheres of impetuous fare
we could possibly conclude.
Without occupying discrepancy

between what distinguished
a fine alto sax sound
from a flute's melodic altruistic pitch.

(We had found the means
of walking to the beat
of our own drummer.)

What It Does

We bleed for attachment,
as soon as we are suspended
from the fold.
Its safety makes us feel whole.
The rush the clan presents
condones the directions
of our assumptions
and assents to vague hypothesis
however, flawed they are.

The soul moreover
professes not to attest
due to distress
when good is arrested
and incapable of contesting
the rights of the pious heart
standing as always on thin ice.

Had it the focus to be disdainful,
arrogant and petulant.
The threat of force
the clan discharges
would have little hope
of subjugating its under armor
for seconds and hours of unity
and alleged understanding
of the disciple's degrading position.

Being a hanger-on
day after day

became years,
class reunions,
and later a 20-year anniversary
of fool-hardiness and non-accomplishment
marked by disrespect
and informal subjugation

I always stood apart from gangs.
I had little if any need to belong
to a singular imposed entity
outside of family.
In our present world,
cliques represent gangs
in whatever make up they are,
clubs, special interests,
Democrats, Republicans, and so on.

Mostly it's like representing like
for the sake of power, influence and prestige.
It has been an ongoing disease.
The cure yet to be found.
We continue to go-round and round
complaining in the absence of the fix
between truth and lies
or greed and mercy.
Perhaps we will discover before our last day.
The value of charity, understanding
and the kindness
insured in the good heart.

Love Did Cast a Frown

She bit my heart,
and I was sick with love.
Unrefined though it was—
precious nonetheless.

I flew without moderation
to meet Icarus' fate.
The euphoric solicitation
of my giggling heart
exposed in triumphant exaltation.

I am made in the image of God.
My breath escaped me.
Her dark eyes consumed me.
They spoke the language
of the new day
for the life irresistibly claimed,
filled with a purpose, lacking shame.

Her untamed juices of creation
endorsed my plate
imposing themselves
with suitable effervescence.

She tried lifting me
from my hangover state.
My helpless heart
of late pierced by a stake.
I had submitted to dreary nights

instead of the cloudless skies,
posting starry constellations.
The North Star was there cheering—
ever the beacon for the embattled wonderer.

Beholding her elegant allure
in every feature,
she was unblurred.
She was demure.
Deleting the cry of a lonely heart's ache
attempted avenues to digress
from misery's prying,
sniffing to add to her distress.
(For these agitations to succeed,
ask for an awkward jest.)

Her symmetrical lips
quoted me a costly undying overture
representing the unknown.
I was led undoubtedly
to shave the hair from my chin
releasing parts of the old me
into the dust filled wind
to show the gains of desperation
before the breast is stabbed deeply
with a bull knife.
(The fog quipped absurdly.)

Her perpetual warmth with commotion
reported their dis-unification
swallowed in one gulp.
(It wasn't too hard for her living anymore
where we cuddled and squatted
on the white sheepskin rug
covering the bedroom floor.)

Mother, Mother

The gravity of her discharge
presented her with an immense task.
She was dated in this world.
Obliged, however, to inquiry
to withhold no service
to self-same acquainted biology
but foster its sustenance.

The designated delirium blunted her,
cast bullets at her.
Led pellets earnestly insisted she capitulate.
Usually they took the form of nasty demands
against the torn green raincoat roving mercifully
corner to corner mercurially.
The American Band
shouted with its drums
entering the town.
The precocious screaming beat
got your heart and feet
marching up and down,
breaking the rules of silence
in the quaint hamlet.

There was little one can do
or would not do when prompted.
Resisting the call only perforated
and underscored the need it sanctions.

Prerecorded

I am of the day
rather than the unseemly restless night
hoping for some company
to guide me
through blustery draped
deceived conventional
obstructed viewpoints.

("Where is my Cleopatra,
the mother of the Nile?")
I wanted her overflow
to saturate me
with rich abundant silt
from her shores.
I wanted to be her king
who can bring valuable goods
and speak of satisfaction.

The peace she gave
must and cannot surcease.
Less the tower,
the one primary pillar
upholding the world
crumbled onto its bleeding knees.

We were bred to accept
the mystery of mysteries,
the Virginal Mother,
whose heart reamed us,
clutched us as our truest trust.

In our very beginning,
We were the babies
who fell and screeched loudly.

Yet before our end
becoming men and women
we erected ourselves
and delivered the best we had to give
the love she granted us
without pause each day.

Mother, you were the conduit
of spiritual peace.
It strengthens our frail goodness
with a healthy dose
of agape's love insisting
we rallied
and tracked every unforced movement
of your smile passing bye.
It said to us, "Be not afraid,
"I can eclipse the sun,
blot out the moon and the stars.
"I will travel with you
until the sounds of your life,
fall still.
"My heart carries with it
only a mother's goodwill."
"Once, again a child,
I cried."

This time her soft words,
went mute,
and both pairs of dark eyes
sealed shut.

Grab Hold

She is no tread bare lily
nor dilly dolly.
Her clout is of a Mustang Sally
the rugged winsome prairie roamer
not seen above
the spine of sloping hills or
the crest of mountain peaks.

Her trail ways lead
us to meet on a cool Sunday morning,
while I stood alongside the blackish pavement
observing the customary splashing sounds
of the river falls.
Quieted in the summer and autumn
by huge closed iron gates.

The geese above had just flown by.
Their speculative noise
offered a friendly intrusion.
Her voice alerted me when she paused.
The incursion was armed with the expression
of shifting delectation
shown in the sheen upon her face.
(More was there offered.)

Her body's physical accents
began interpreting its bustle.
The clamoring of her arms and legs

expanded the message.
They read like a diary of sensuous revelations.

Both of us provoked and goaded,
opposed the slightest ebb.

The intervention was a meal
consumed with nuclear intent.
The explosion rented
beauty's acclaimed attitude
filled with audacious pulsations.

Had her sleek figure
been adorned by four decades
of rioting.
It still would be loyal to those years
and not discriminate
as it was meant to otherwise.
To do an about face, say bye
voiced the unconstitutional lie.
The query's needed was not
to halt its song
below the navel button.

To be with someone,
a man or woman
made the candied taste of life work.

What came after the splash
can be a spiteful hurt
with one's muddy mask in the muck,
spitting blood
from the storm of reinstated liability.

"Hello," she said, to me.
Her hailing grounded me instantaneously.
My tree roots clutched the mud
sinking deeper and deeper.
Their lively insistence
felt the tickle of lascivious intents
declaring their raging sentiment.
(Sacrifice deplores lament.)

Her esoteric bohemian spirit
filled me with the intricate complication
of both happiness and sadness
folded into one.
Her appearance brought a significant
departure to my pastoral orderliness.
It spiked ten degrees!

The birth of our invited discernment
let self-reproach cast aside
the apology of anguish.

We extended ourselves
glowing towards each other
akin to the princely friends; we were
who knew there was no end in sight
and didn't wish it.
Less we stumbled
and lost the grip we had
the same as a man
and an attractive woman
in a dark room
who thought themselves innocent.
(Who needs be such fools
to condemn what rules,
the caverns of their tools?)

A Dream Returned

You could be the way
my mother was.

Her pleasing footsteps
were an orchestrated chorale
unceasing in her routine's bevy of activity.
At first buzzing near bye,
then drifting silently away,
the black stripe bumble bee
monitored the four rooms.

She swished her wicker-broom.
It danced restlessly
across the dusty floors,
then paused
for the pots and pans
to rattle and clink in the sink.
She scrubbed them
until their outer rims shined.
and prayed she left
those dull days behind.
(It came sooner than her thoughts knew)
sooner than we, her young sons
had time to grow up by her side.)
(The castle was always cleaned
of every minute rubble.)

She would perform
the same tasks tomorrow.

The house always qualified
to accommodate a visitor.
Pride in your work is everything.)
A common but noble affair
before her lingering end raised
the drawbridge to all
who formerly entered her small dominion.

Her visage now was cloudy to me
explained only by one black and white
polaroid photograph,
an ancient scientific miracle
from ages and ages passed.
It captured her rounded cheekbone edges,
and the beige,
amber chestnut highlights
of her completion.
With a click, the regal tenderness
existing in motherhood was memorialized.

These unique women
wielded the title, mother,
owned this exclusive power.
It took hold of them.
They extended it without hesitation
day after day.

With this staff,
you as well
gloriously purchased my soul
with your extraordinary luster
exuding calmly through
your copper colored eyes
held beneath striking raven hair
draped two feet below your shoulder blade.

Prerecorded

Images such as these were tokens,
priceless heirlooms
for the mind to visit,
and the heart's treasure to recapture
whenever doldrums
dumped a touch of misrepresented moping.

Your face in my head
gently slipped me into sleep
the same as my mother did.

I snuck a peep
and released a smile
when I felt the squeeze
of her warm hug.

You were mom, the shield
that guarded against looming wounds
to those too weak to deflect yet
the blows living will offer.

I Swear to God

I swear to God.
I swear to God
to release the pounding
in my head.
The childish thief causes
by stripping love of its charity
and the passion
that yearns to deploy its shafts
of meaningful altruism.

Irreverence she lets fly
with casual callousness.
A reminder of the big black
New Hampshire flies
biting my arms and legs
on those humid mountain
sticky July summer days.

Painful swelling follows
their beastly attacks upon
the night's sleep made absent any peace.

Had I been a stranger calling
with empathy and concern in tow
disturbed over the violent impact,
her axe took to
cleave my head in half
and plow its way

through the middle of my chest.
I am quickly made a cadaver.
Butchered and tossed on a metal table.
Gristle and bones,
blood and skin on display
for the garbage barrel.

The years of sacrifice,
the years of haunting concerns,
the years of apprehensions,
the hopeful desire,
immaturity mutates
into serious sensibility,
storing production of love's happiness
instead of nesting in the carriage
of brutish disdain.

In an abrupt acute word,
I bring to grapple
with a sour verbal upheaval.
She confined in her narrow-minded minority
is a child blinded,
unwilling to reflect
how to serve someone else's need.
(Call it an absence of respect or disrespect.)

The jarring in my head,
the pounding, the pushing,
the pulling in all direction
is rage shaking
the iron bars of its cage.

I swear to God madness circles.
Its use a shovel and a pick

inscribed a marble stone
that states,
"Love suffered much
and died from such."

I swear to God.
Heed not my call,
if should tomorrow
I fall into my grave
her obtuse behavior
be dismissed, forgotten,
its pain showered, will not visit
another she chooses
to address with such
a lack of cultured generosity.
Their time together will mold.
They'll mourn—eventually disown
their appraisal's worth.
His heart like mine turns to stone.
She will find herself dissolved from her bones
when he departs from her days.
Her sorrows will rise,
dance merrily atop her grave.

Children make sharp indifferent stakes
and push them deeply into the minds
and spirit, their parents must forsake.
They use ignoble utterances,
think themselves clever,
without considering
the outrageous damage done
with their pestilence.
The meanness defaces inherently
the excellence the soul transfer to life.

I swear to God.
I am sorry to have used
Your Holy Name so poorly.
I am ashamed to have made the claim.

Perhaps tomorrow
I'll not have cause
for such an alarm.
Perhaps tomorrow
I'll not be so disarmed.

As a brash young boy,
often, I acted thusly,
spoke irreverently when profoundly annoyed.
My father always forgave me
with each new day's arrival.
I am washed clean from my sludge,
and we begin again as friends.

Something I should always recall
in light, of his teaching
with the next sunrise.

The only permanence is in change,
which comes with age.
 I followed its search since youth.

I choose not to waste
nor hurt my days left
by shunning her,
and the gleeful experiences
that is the joy
a child had yet to bestow.

Together We

You came to my world,
wild, free, aglow
and glowed,
like the brilliant sun high above
your face, a brilliant Aegean Sun
the choice of the watchful gods,
ever vigilant.
I took my chance.
My heart was challenged by you.
I was as Achilles motivated
to conquer the Trojans.
Skill and passion
commanded their walls to fall.
Your splendid heart made me a warrior.
Absorbed, I seized the precious jewel.

Our tale began.
Tears arose telling it,
since beauty has the means
to make us scream
in between heaven and earth
and bereft
when your loss provided us
its most selfish test.
She had just entered her start in life.
Her instinctive flourishing sang
through the seams of music
appearing in the throes of art.

Prerecorded

She made our minds go beyond
where comfort need not go
to indulge comfort's sake.
Her sight allowed us that peek.
The streaks through sunset's golden clouds
accentuated the radiance of your vibrant hues.
The spread was like
the NBC's peacock's tail.

I felt you then in my soul.
You extolled what I beheld:
life free,
a gypsy's dance,
an evening's prance
savage fun.
Going here and there—
going where you were meant to be seen.
The world made you an invitation,
and you grabbed it, boldly.
You were the red shinny fruit
hanging from the apple tree.

My teeth would risk taking a bite
if in my lap you fell.

One day I will accompany you,
and we will walk and talk.
The months for us
will evade becoming powder ash.
We'll not see our dream's end
but contest, pose and be addressed.

Together, as before,
our hearts we pledged
ceasing to be cold and alone.

Prerecorded

Your love was there to be won.
I found its heat;
its power made me weak.

I wept while you slept
from you I did not break
nor you from me at the wake.

Someday together we'll accompany
each other and again
live in God's holy retreat.

The Hold

Michaelanne wrapped herself
around our bones.
Covered our stranded souls
with her artistic fingers
capable of producing
heart-warming, miraculous design,
equal to a marvelous Madonna.
A Christmas gift we anticipated; its discovery
below the blue spruce evergreen tree, someday.

When received,
our spirits will inflame.
Though now we instinctively know,
the Lord has made our world a better place.

Each day of her life
we felt her nature's grace,
a gentle embrace
to brighten our path
with its fountain's unending
outburst of love.
The purest sacrifice
ultimately given.

For her a certain kind of love
was yet to arrive.
In her heart, its magic was stored
to reward the humble prince

destined to unveil
her treasure chest of mystical wonders
adept at suppling the status
of her visual art's dominance.

Being late
for this date
with fate,
mocked a dream.
Before the princes' arrival,
there was much felicity
in the numerous,
distinctive friendships
with those who were blessed
to partake in her wonder.

She was the fortune
bestowed us
in the resplendence
of an Easter morning sunrise.

Seeing her face glistening
at the distant end of the road,
my heart is moved to console,
to revoke her death.

Catch the Moment

Catch the catered times of your life
when you can.
Soon, you'll be old
and not able to catch anymore
of them quite as easily.
This autumn sunny Sunday morning
conveniently hands her over
as a target of opportunity.

To my left, on her right,
she approaches straight forwardly.
Fifteen meters, ten meters away
I dip my head not wanting to glare
at her oncoming slightly fulfilling figure
in snug blue jeans, silk puffy pink scarf,
and the contrasting blue ski jacket.
The low stylish red dotted converse sneakers
and white sox I think warmed her toes
from the frosty twenty-one blustery degrees.

At five meters, I could see plainly
her brown coiffured hair style
and grey eyes
before me. She blinked twice
and held me in place.

With an abrupt decisive diagonal step,
she catches me off guard.

Fight or flight takes over.
I hedge to my right
uttering only an anemic, "Hello,"
rather than an energic
intreating salutation filled question,
"Do you like poetry?"
That could have stalled her enough
to give us a genesis.

Hearing my unsteady word,
she smiles, nods, retracts
her direction straight at me
and starts to disappear
in the distance beyond me.

I slowed my onward progress.
Turning my head and shoulders
halfway around,
I take an accurate and hindmost look
at her richly etched thighs from the stern.
They have much to say going away.

Our trail separating
is a poor triumph
against the unlikely future endeavor
I hope with her to undertake.

Heraclitus said,
"You cannot step into the same river twice."

Though if such happens, I would surely yell,
"Your beauty has kindness enshrined in it.
Its imperative compels me
to never again this close to you,

deny myself at least a few
hundred yards of conversations
with a crown jewel."

On this earth, while we wait,
we must perform
and trust the outcome
of our chances.
Time and favorable junctures
permit us to avoid falling prey
to snowballing avalanches,
a broken leg, a cracked body
alone to mend.
I had the opportunity
but let fear run my race
and I was (DQ) disqualified.

The Long March Home (Redux)

Our story didn't stop
but marched like an army
bent on achieving eternal joy
at each other's side.
We traveled far and wide
ending in the blessed shadow
of the Great Spirit
where we both blissfully glowed.

"With all the love I own,
this I give to thee,"
said he, smiling at her once youthful face.
That we with eyes and wings
like turtle doves look-down from above.
Her peaceful expression replies
with a crystal sigh,
"The good I have is your doing."

About the Author

Stephen Pitters is a leader in the arts' community, a teacher of words, and a confidant to many. Pitters uses a brash voice to release his emotions, but he also uses an intimate voice to serenade his lovers or to lullaby his children. He doesn't aspire to the usual: he's unique in his writing and in his ability to articulate matters of the soul into poetry. He is an outsider; he doesn't pretend to fit in with other contemporary, institutional, or commercial poets. His work spans the language and the sentiment in the orbit of past canonical pillars such as John Donne or Percy Bysshe Shelley. Pitters brings a spiritual component to his romantic memoir in poetry. He expresses how God and fate play into the recounting of his life. Additionally, these poems chronicle his years as an African-American man who becomes entangled with many inamoratas who are either passing infatuations or longer, love-struck relationships. Often, Pitters strips down to his raw emotions as he pines for past passions. He sets the temporal tone with the use of language some consider archaic, while Pitters recognizes the beauty and the utility of these words as nostalgic connotations. This is the fifth collection of poetry in the series.

Made in the USA
Columbia, SC
03 April 2018